Much more than a summary of *The Sopranos*, the legendary cable-TV game-changer, this sequence of prose poems presents an interior monologue in the voice of Tony Soprano, spoken in second-person by Tony's meditative self, as if in a fugue state in his shrink's office, or better, writing it all down in a notebook, to save his life. Its 86 intense word-packages (prose, but never prosaic) present the spit on which all bodies turn: loyalty, depression, angst, love, lust, sentimentality, courage—and, rarely, a break in the clouds: '… [B]reathe in the reassuring smells of cigar smoke and dried manure and fresh hay. Tomorrow you'll collect outstanding debts. Not today.' I found no false step here in the language; these poems are cut and polished, and absolutely in character. More than a remarkable book, it's a thrilling one. The humor is mordant ('You suspect the Chicken Vindaloo was actually Cocker Spaniel'), the language sharply varying from imagistic ('flush with crackheads' small bills') to a staccato-Hammett 'cracking wise' ('Come on: he can only play that poor-me, ex-con cousin card so long'), to thoughts too deep for words, where waves crashing on the beach bring memories of those you've whacked and sunk in chains. This is a comic masterpiece, which is to say, it's a tragedy, too.

—James Cummins, author of *Still Some Cake, Then and Now,* and *The Whole Truth*

Like a
Soprano

poems by

David Starkey

SERVING HOUSE BOOKS

Like a Soprano

ISBN: 978-0-9913281-8-5

Cover photograph: "Skyway Diner" by Mark Hillringhouse

"In the "Full Leather Jacket" episode (#21) Christopher Moltisanti (played by Michael Imperioli) was shot in front of the Skyway Diner, seen here. His shooters, Matt Bevalaqua and Sean Gismonte, both now sleep with the fishes." (Filming Locations from 'The Sopranos')

Author photo by Patricia Houghton Clarke

Serving House Books logo by Barry Lereng Wilmont

Published by Serving House Books
Copenhagen, Denmark and Florham Park, NJ
www.servinghousebooks.com

Member of The Independent Book Publishers Association

First Serving House Books Edition 2014

Thanks to the editors of *Askew Magazine*, where several of the poems in this book first appeared.

For James Gandolfini
1961-2013

Sometimes I go about in pity for myself,
and all the while a great wind carries me across the sky.
　—Ojibwe proverb

'I liked that,' said Offa, 'sing it again.'
　—Geoffrey Hill, *The Mercian Hymns*

Poetry Collections by David Starkey

Koan Americana
Open Mike Night at the Cabaret Voltaire
Ways of Being Dead
Adventures of the Minor Poet
A Few Things You Should Know About the Weasel
It Must Be Like the World
Circus Maximus

Contents

1

The Sopranos   15
46 Long   16
Denial, Anger, Acceptance   17
Meadowlands   18
College   19
Pax Soprana   20
Down Neck   21
The Legend of Tennessee Moltisanti   22
Boca   23
A Hit Is a Hit   24
Nobody Knows Anything   25
Isabella   26
I Dream of Jeannie Cusamano   27

2

Guy Walks into a Psychiatrist's Office...   31
Do Not Resuscitate   32
Toodle Fucking-Oo   33
Commendatori   34
Big Girls Don't Cry   35
The Happy Wanderer   36
D-Girl   37
Full Leather Jacket   38
From Where to Eternity   39
Bust Out   40
House Arrest   41
The Knight in White Satin Armor   42
Funhouse   43

3

Mr. Ruggiero's Neighborhood   47
Proshai, Livushka   48
Fortunate Son   49
Employee of the Month   50
Another Toothpick   51
University   52
Second Opinion   53
He Is Risen   54
The Telltale Moozadell   55
...To Save Us All from Satan's Power   56
Pine Barrens   57
Amour Fou   58
Army of One   59

4

For All Debts Public and Private   63
No Show   64
Christopher   65
The Weight   66
Pie-O-My   67
Everybody Hurts   68
Watching Too Much Television   69
Mergers and Acquisitions   70
Whoever Did This   71
The Strong, Silent Type   72
Calling All Cars   73
Eloise   74
Whitecaps   75

5

Two Tonys   79
Rat Pack   80

Where's Johnny?   81
All Happy Families...   82
Irregular Around the Margins   83
Sentimental Education   84
In Camelot   85
Marco Polo   86
Unidentified Black Males   87
Cold Cuts   88
The Test Dream   89
Long Term Parking   90
All Due Respect   9.1

6.1

Members Only   95
Join the Club   96
Mayham   97
The Fleshy Part of the Thigh   98
Mr. & Mrs. John Sacrimoni Request...   99
Live Free or Die   100
Luxury Lounge   101
Johnny Cakes   102
The Ride   103
Moe n' Joe   104
Cold Stones   105
Kaisha   106

6.2

Soprano Home Movies   109
Stage 5   110
Remember When   111
Chasing It   112
Walk Like a Man   113
Kennedy and Heidi   114

The Second Coming   115
The Blue Comet   116
Made in America   117

1

The Sopranos

The wild ducks have flown from your North Jersey swimming pool—
away from the panic attacks and goomars in sailors' caps, beyond
the garbage mounds and pigs' heads hung by hooks, the hundreds
stashed in Campbell's soup cans, the men wound as tightly as the
rope around a snitch's wrists.

Your mother never loved you. Your uncle wants to kill you. Your
daughter's getting high.

You gaze out the window like a boy who's lost his father. Breadcrumbs
sink into the warm, chlorinated water.

Ah, Jesus, fuck, now he's going to cry.

46 Long

Everything has gone to hell.

Made men are spilling secrets on talk shows. The culture's been raped
of its cappuccino, calzone and buffalo mozzarella. Your old mad
mother doesn't want your delphiniums, though they come from
Frankie Valli's personal florist.

The fire's never friendly.

The barman at the strip club can't figure out how to work the phone.

And yet there is still time to crack wise with colleagues while drinking
Scotch and sorting through grocery bags of cash, time to watch *The
Bank Dick* on DVD, then browse a truckload of stolen Italian suits
looking for something classy in your size.

Denial, Anger, Acceptance

The Jews and Romans are at war again. This time, the spoils are a twenty-five percent stake in the Fly Away Motel. His side curls against your brass knuckles. Talmudic law versus a gold crucifix on a delicate gold chain.

A rabbi can transform a golem from mud to sentient clay, but God only can snuff the inhuman creature if it's a mind to stay alive.

And so the *capo dei capi*'s hair has begun falling out as he shrinks into his hospital gown, calling for the nurse to take his temperature again.

Meadowlands

Your nephew in a neck brace, son in a school fight, wife raging with discontent.

Your psychiatrist equips you with strategies for coping, but you make syndicate decisions in a lobster bib, swallow Xanax as the strippers pivot on their poles.

Nevertheless, because elders cherish the childish illusion of control, you placate you mother with macaroons, bend a knee to Uncle Junior, watching as the old man in his feathered fedora receives tribute in a graveyard overrun by turnpike noise.

College

Your daughter is a straight "A" student. You tell her she could be one of
the models right out of Italian *Vogue*. Whereto, the private colleges
of Maine await: Colby, Bowdoin, Bates.

One tiny matter first: you must waste the ratfuck who flipped. It's
tricky, though, like the cat-and-mouse game your wife plays with the
priest she's crushing on, Father Phil, who's jonesing for her baked
ziti.

Finally, you find him unready, strangle him with an extension cord until
his eyes bulge as wide as the vainglorious New England sky.

Pax Soprana

The Prozac's breaking your balls. For Christ's sake, you want to *talk*
    with your goomar.

Even though your shrink—in her beige suits and skirts—is colorless,
    you love her. She listens.

It's a lesson you're trying to teach your uncle, newly crowned: Augustus
    Caesar never ate alone.

Down Neck

Your son sneaks into the church and gets drunk on sacramental wine.
Suddenly, it's ADD this, a complete battery of testing that. Your
wife's punishment: no Mario Kart or skateboarding for three weeks.

What happened to the days when a kid got out of line and his
father could play a little tarantella on his head? Back in the old
neighborhood, when your mother threatened to stab a fork in your
eye, she was simply making a point.

Alas, the consolations of the past are few.

You forgive your son by feeding him whipped cream from an aerosol
can.

The Legend of Tennessee Moltisanti

Your nephew dreams of pork and corpses returned from moldering in
the marshes. Spectral warnings.

He wants to write a screenplay, but he's having trouble with the
dialogue. The action, not so much.

Tennessee Williams was not a made man, though surely he understood
the gangster's maxim: the more people you kill, the easier you sleep.

Also, if the baker takes too long to serve your cannoli and Napoleons,
sometimes you have to shoot him in the foot.

Boca

Your wife learns through nail parlor gossip that your uncle's time in
Florida is spent whistling in the wheat field. He's like a great artist,
his girlfriend tells him—he has a real instinct for it.

But muff diving won't fly in Belleville. Nothing extraordinary will.
Shamed, the old man can no longer face the woman to whom he
once gave such pleasure.

Sometimes this place depresses you, despite the Prozac with a Lord
Calvert chaser.

A Hit Is a Hit

Charity be damned: no matter how many boxes of Monte Cristo
    Cuban cigars you allocate, you'll always be the token gangster to the
    Wonder Bread Wops at the country club.

You can almost sympathize with the soul singers your pal the Jewish
    loanshark ripped off all those lifetimes ago.

Or the kid with the cleft palate who sang "Mack the Knife" to his
    friends but cried himself to sleep.

Or the knucklehead who tried to grill a trout with a downed power line:
    being electrocuted turned his life around.

Maybe even, just for a moment, you can see yourself as the Columbian
    drug dealer with a hole in his head, flush with crackheads' small
    bills.

Nobody Knows Anything

Big Pussy's flipped, busted moving H to pay his kids' tuition. So says
the crooked cop with a gambling problem and a suicidal bent, a few
days away from taking a header off the Route 1 Bridge.

But you don't trust him, and you don't clip a friend when you're ninety
percent sure. You wait until you see the wire strapped on his body.
Understand? You wait until you yourself are almost dead.

Isabella

What are the chances of the most beautiful dental exchange student in
the world moving in next door when you are Lithium-soaked and
disconsolate, shambling through the house in your bathrobe, lower
than a junkie who's sold his kid to score?

She's the tenderhearted mother you never had, her voice like church
bells ringing, her breath a lemon-scented breeze.

But she's just a fantasy, a trigger to jolt you from your torpid state back
to the reality of bullets and betrayal.

Those tiny tears will dry in autumn wind.

I Dream of Jeannie Cusamano

The priest's a schnorrer and a schumuck.

Your shrink has split to keep from getting clipped.

And yet they continue to appear, like visions to a saint, those little
moments you can cherish: a candlelight dinner with your family in
Nuovo Vesuvio; finally confronting your mother on all her filicidal
bullshit; wrapping a corpse in chains and cinder blocks and sinking
it to the bottom of the bay; dreaming of your neighbor's wife.

2

Guy Walks into a Psychiatrist's Office...

Your shrink's still on the lam, seeing patients in a motel room. When you follow her to a roadside diner and ask to recommence, she refuses. Car reflections flash in the stainless steel creamer. Traffic noise works its way through the windowpanes.

Your nephew's playing stockbroker, cold-calling seniors, pumping and dumping.

Big Pussy's back, with a half-assed tale about Percocets and some Puerto Rican broad.

And then here comes your sister, Parvati Wasatch, aka Janice, drawing disability for the carpal tunnel syndrome she picked up working the espresso machine at a Seattle coffeehouse. Your father's favorite, she's not through blighting your life.

At least you still have home cooking. Your wife heats up cold pasta in the microwave. At the kitchen table, you eat quietly, but with an appetite, while she sifts grimly through the family bills.

Do Not Resuscitate

Growing old is hell—for other people. Family histories, memories of
war.

Your uncle under house arrest, ankle bracelet hard as a turtle's carapace.
After the old man slips in the shower and cracks his hip, you must
carry him like a child to the car.

In unmarked envelopes, unhallowed sheaves of cash. Midnight like
Judgment Day.

Your sour-tongued mother still snug in her hospital bed after she
gave the nod to whack you. On the boombox—a gift from her
daughter—Pavarotti warbling *"Non ti scordar di me."*

Toodle Fucking-Oo

Now, your psychiatrist is crushing on *you*. She confesses to her own therapist that she's regressing to a ditzy young girl.

Your daughter wrecks your mother's empty house. Ecstasy and ambulances. Candles in beer bottles, and barf on the hardwood floors. The punishment: three weeks without her Discover card.

Richie Aprile's back from ten years in the can. He wants his cut, and he'll smash a glass coffee decanter against the skull of anyone who demurs. Fuck that, he'll run the motherless fuck over in his SUV.

Your own life proceeds apace. Red wine in restaurants. A box of honeycombs. A showdown in the Garden State Plaza mall.

Commendatori

In Napoli, you devour prawns in a harbor restaurant, dodge trash on
the beach, sip amaretto while cutting deals. *You are your own worst
enemy*, says your Southern Italian counterpart, a woman so alluring
she might be the Sibyl of Cumae.

Your self-loathing wife also is a foe, never a partner but always an accessory—
imagining evening sun shimmering on the Mediterranean as she
simmers tomato sauce on the stove.

And then Jimmy Bones, expendable Elvis impersonator about to have
his brains bashed in with a ball-peen hammer: he should never have
asked those questions of Big Pussy in the party store.

And Furio Giunta, the Neapolitan hatchet man hauled back to Jersey
for no good end: where, now, is his war?

Big Girls Don't Cry

Acting is mostly feeling, says your nephew's acting coach. *What do you want to achieve here?*

For starters, how about a little recognition? How about someone paying what they owe?

Your wife tells you to grow the fuck up, but your psychiatrist wants you back. She thinks treating you will be therapeutic...for her.

You're okay with that. First, though, you must send Furio into a whorehouse with a baseball bat, after which you steal an hour to bang your goomar on your boat, the *Stugots.*

Yet for all your shouting and ripping phones from walls, you're like the rest of us: you just want to tell someone your dreams.

The Happy Wanderer

Let this be a lesson in risk management: how your high school friend
was drawn magnetically to cigar smoke and poker chips; potato
chips and provolone; the nine of spades; trip deuces; three beautiful
kings; this fucking guy who will not stop when he's ahead but
ambles back into trouble like a stray cat wandering onto the New
Jersey Turnpike in the rain; this *chooch* you want to smash in the face
with a fucking brick.

Gamblers always lose.

D-Girl

Nietzsche was right, your son and mother concur: God is dead, and life's
    a futile, solitary mess.

Thus, your nephew's big break with the development girl lasts only as
    long as she can milk his story for the studio. The star's gone west to
    Hollywood.

At your son's Confirmation party, unhappiness is rife. Twilight of the
    idols.

What your family needs is a good scolding, a little less braggadocio. The
    young man—fresh from his catechism, the laying on of hands—is
    high in the garage. Big Pussy, miked for double-dealing, is sobbing
    in the powder room.

Stay tuned: the story is unfolding.

Full Leather Jacket

Your nephew can crack a safe with a crowbar, buy his disaffected
girlfriend's love with a three-carat diamond ring.

Two douchebags later, though, he's lying in the street, spent bullet
casings on wet concrete near his bleeding head.

From Where to Eternity

Impulses gnostic and anagogic surge through the imminently bereft.

Your nephew sleeps in a hospital bed, a medallion of Pope John Paul II resting shepherdly on his chest. Behold, a vision: Hell is an Irish bar where every day's St. Paddy's Day, and every mobster inclines in that direction.

One of your capos, Paulie Gualtieri, seeks a Nyack psychic who, in his well-appointed living room, perceives the men that Paulie's whacked.

You choose, wisely, to ignore prophecy.

Your wife says she wants only you, and only wants you to be true. A host of ceramic angels hover on her bedside table as you pledge to one another a rare night of love.

Bust Out

Webern's *Variations for Piano* quavers on the stereo as a good citizen
realizes the man he saw while hiding in ragweed that night was boss
of the New Jersey mob. The notes, off-kilter and harsh, skitter and
stot around his living room when he calls the cops to recant.

In the mean season, you and your cronies have busted out the sporting
goods store you won at cards—every line of credit is as spent as
an old *puttana*. The owner, your high school friend, is sleeping in
a tent on the half-empty floor, drunk and lorn and weeping. He
made his bed....

In celebration of your witness's disavowal, you allow your feckless son
to steer the *Stugots* down the Shark River. Its wake capsizes two
palookas manning a canoe, but you take no notice. Your gaze is
fixed on the Atlantic's cloud-bound horizon.

House Arrest

Your shrink's cup-shotten, getting loaded between sessions on Belvedere,
   arguing in restaurants with other dyspeptic diners.

Your uncle's under house arrest; an oxygen mask; a knack for
   disremembering; his hand stuck in the kitchen drain for hours.

You're practically on the peg yourself, trapped behind a desk at Barone
   Sanitation while the Feds are on your ass—drawing goldfish on a
   legal pad, conjoining with the secretary.

Fuck it: let them catch you if they can. You're soon back smoking a
   stogie outside Satriale's. *Chicken Parts: Order Here. Baby Lamb
   Chops. Italian Sausage: 1.99 a pound.*

The Knight in White Satin Armor

Once he's testified and does his time, Big Pussy wants to join the FBI.
    He's already on the case, following your crew on their way to jack a
    truckload of Pokémon cards.

But Puss is an idiot, like everybody else. A car wreck of a man.

It's all just one more imbroglio for you, the scepter-state, to untangle.

Look at your Russian mistress, so desperate for affection she'd consider
    declining a fat envelope of *scharole.*

And your sister, fugitive again after two clean shots into the heart of her
    lover, Rolling Stones' tattoo conspicuous on her capacious chest.

You're almost ready to agree with your hated mother's considered
    opinion of the human family. Cruelty is all we can count on. *Babies
    are like animals.*

Funhouse

You suspect the chicken vindaloo was actually Cocker Spaniel. Now it's
a night and day of vomiting and fever and dreams, dreams, dreams.

Snow on the boardwalk. The shops all closed. Wind creaks the wooden
slats. You want to light yourself on fire.

Life: the Big Nothing. Even Madame Marie couldn't have predicted
Big Pussy would metamorphose into a talking sea bass to confess his
sins.

Dragging yourself from bed, you and two trusted capos steal a boat
and coax the ratfuck out to sea. You honor Pussy's last request not
to be shot in the face, but plug him everywhere else. As seagulls
shriek their vain complaints, the three of you wrap him in a tarp and
chains and roll him into the swell.

This boardwalk life is through: your family celebrates your daughter's
high school graduation, but you're distracted, sparking a cigar,
contemplating the coming darkness.

Waves pound the beach at Asbury Park.

3

Mr. Ruggiero's Neighborhood

Every morning when you walk down your driveway in bathrobe and
   skivvies to pick up the *Star-Ledger*, the Feds are hovering. With
   Big Pussy dead, they have a warranted sneak-and-peak to bug your
   basement.

It's a complicated affair, tailing Mr. and Mrs. Bing, and your children,
   Baby and Princess, across your tangled schedules, but finally the
   wire's live.

Motherfuck. The water heater blows; the plumber, Mr. Ruggiero, is
   called; and the Feds must start all over.

This time it's a dummy lamp, tucked in among the mildewy crap on the
   workbench, and the tapes are rolling.

Now, twenty-four hours a day, in their Montclair Transport van, they
   listen to your family's clap and glaver. You tell your wife the coffee's
   been good lately. She tells you that you need more roughage in your
   diet.

Proshai, Livushka

Your daughter's brought home a boyfriend from Columbia: half-Jewish, half-*ditsoon*. Word to the wise: that box of Uncle Ben's rice may now trigger a panic attack.

Meanwhile, your mother dies as you're moving the sprinkler on your back lawn.

Her funeral's awkward. The wake is even worse.

If only you'd had Jimmy Cagney's mama in *Public Enemy*—gray hair a frizzy friendly nest, her breasts comfortable old pillows. Now there was an old lady worth toasting to, in Russian, or any other tongue.

Fortunate Son

It's all coming back to you now in therapy: that night your father
    slashed off Satriale's pinky for an unpaid debt, then brought home
    a pot roast to your mother. It was so succulent, a beautiful cut.
    When she dipped her pinky in the juice then dipped that same
    finger in your father's mouth, they began dancing, close, while your
    father sang "All of Me."

Before they finished, you had passed out on the kitchen floor.

Employee of the Month

The chain of custody has failed and now Jesus Rossi, the man who raped your psychiatrist in the empty stairwell of a parking garage, is free to return to his job at WrapNation Subway Sandwiches, where his picture hangs on the wall.

The other men in her life are worthless. Thus, she faces a dilemma: tell you, her guardian gangster angel, and become your debtor, or brave the woe herself.

In session, she begins to weep. Solicitous, you ask if you can help. She thinks hard. Her lacerated knee is screaming, her cheek is bruised, her jaw is swollen. She stares at you with unblinking virid eyes.

No.

Another Toothpick

Everybody knows bad things come in threes: cops and courts and cancer.

The Cedar Grove flatfoot with a hard-on for fair play. You bust his balls so hard he winds up working weekends at Fountains of Wayne.

Your Uncle Junior trapped in his wood-paneled living room, watching soaps as his trial looms like the heart attack lurking in a plate of ossobucco smothered with risotto and fried zucchini flowers.

And crazy Baccalieri Senior, hacking blood into a handkerchief just before he blows his godson's brains against the ceiling. It's proud work, his final hit—despite his carcinoma-riddled lungs, he rewards himself with a Marlboro Light, and then another.

University

Your daughter gets dumped in the Columbia library. The boy—the *mulignan* you hate—finds her too negative; her OCD roommate's a major pest.

She'll never tell you, of course, which is just as well: you have problems of your own.

The stripper who baked you a loaf of date nut bread has been beaten to death in back of the Bada Bing! She's supine amid a tumble of empty whisky boxes, heaps of trash.

Ralph Cifaretto's an asshole, but a terrific earner. What can you do but slap him around and let him go, while the moon shines down like an eye doctor's penlight, and the air's ripe with sibilance—the rush of traffic, the feculent creek surging through the storm drain, washing her bloody hair.

Second Opinion

Autumn in North Caldwell. Your uncle suffering through
    chemotherapy; your heartsore daughter home every third day for ziti
    with sweet sausage; your nephew a junkie with busted balls.

And your wife…her psychiatrist says leave you; take the children and
    nothing else. Go.

But she's lying on the couch in the middle of the day, wrapped in a floral
    quilt. You ask her if she's sick. She's not. She's not ready. She walks
    upstairs, the quilt draped over her shoulders, and you follow, slowly,
    perplexed—for once in your life unprepared.

He Is Risen

Post-Thanksgiving, Gigi Cestone dies on the crapper of a heart attack, the turkey like spackles in his bowels. Ralph Cifaretto's capo now.

No fucking way, you'd said, just days before, but in this racket things change with Lazarus-like speed.

You know you ought to pause amidst your plotting and reading of Sun Tzu just to listen to the music made by the names of your associates— Johnny Sacrimoni, Eugene Pontecorvo, Vito Spatafore—but there's a new woman in your life. She sells Mercedes. You met her in your doctor's office, so maybe she's a little crazy, but then maybe you are, too.

The Telltale Moozadell

Extra mozzarella on the pizza is the only clue the North Caldwell cops
    need to bust your son and friends for trashing the Verbum Dei
    swimming pool. Lucky for him he's on the football team.

Still, the kid's a shitwit, like Jackie Junior, that lying gangster wannabe
    who brags about his sway and smarts but can't even write a paper on
    Edgar Allen Poe.

You'd wonder why the young men of New Jersey went so far astray, if
    you weren't off course yourself, dancing with your new brainsick
    goomar in a hotel room. She tells you all she wants is kindness,
    though she's fondling the pistol strapped to your ankle as though it
    were your culminating present on Christmas Day.

...To Save Us All from Satan's Power

Seaside, the wind and waves whispering regret, you recall the clipping of
   Big Pussy, and suddenly the panic attacks return.

Your sister, too, is having trouble: none of the Christian songs she and
   her narcoleptic boyfriend have written smack of anything close to a
   hit.

And don't let anyone get you started on Jackie Junior, your daughter's
   new inconstant boyfriend, whose Christmas gift was a necklace
   promising he'd always be true.

This year, even the toy giveaway at Satriale's is shit. *Fuck you, Santa*, a
   gap-toothed boy tells red-suited Bobby Baccala, whose nylon beard's
   askew, his attitude not much better than the kid's.

Pine Barrens

Sometimes things go wrong.

This Russian, he owes Silvio five grand, but Sil's dying with the flu so
   you make a call: your nephew and Paulie Gualtieri must collect.

They drive down to Fair Lawn, but this fucking guy, he's got a mouth
   on him it's hard to believe. Before they know it, they've cracked his
   windpipe with a floor lamp, rolled him into rug and driven him to
   South Jersey.

The new plan is this: bury him in the Barrens, then head to Morton's in
   AC for a steak. At least the day won't be a total loss.

But this fucking guy, he's still alive—turns out he was a commando in
   the Russian army, singlehandedly killed sixteen Chechen rebels—or
   was it Czechoslovakians? He disappears in the woods and, chasing
   him, they soon are lost.

A full moon shines through the pines down on the endless fields of
   snow. Silk suits, silk socks, alligator shoes—in an even-handed
   world they'd freeze to death, but in this one, day dawns and they
   limp into the warmth of your waiting Suburban.

They fucked up, but they're alive, as always. There must be a God
   because otherwise, how explain it?

Amour Fou

Your wife is crying in the Met, hands clasped before Ribera's *Mystical
   Marriage of Saint Catherine.* Marrying a baby—it's sick, but
   somehow it makes sense. All that emotion a woman dons like
   a wedding or a mourning dress. These days, even dog food
   commercials bring her to tears.

She confesses to the priest that her life is financed by crime. He tells her
   to ignore the sin and learn to live on what the good part earns.

But how much could that possibly be, and what *is* the good part when
   your bedlam-ripe goomar is stalking her, then begging you: *Kill me,
   kill me, kill me, kill me.*

Your wife's not crazy, not even pregnant. Her home is comfortably
   appointed. What she thinks she knows, she doesn't really know.

There are worse fates than studying for the real estate exam while
   making lemon snaps for the bake sale at the church.

Army of One

Jackie Junior fucked up heisting the poker game. Now he's holed up
   in the Boonton projects just long enough to realize life is a ballad
   he will not sing. Shot in the back of the head by Vito Spatafore, he
   departs New Jersey face-down in a patch of dirty roadside snow.

Your own son's latest midnight prank has him expelled again, but
   military school's not an option: panic attacks, the family curse.

So, your arm around your son at Jackie Junior's wake, you listen as
   Uncle Junior, your surrogate father, sings *"Core 'ngrato,"* to a room
   where the words resonate.

Look at them: all those tearful, faithless, ungrateful hearts.

4

For All Debts Public and Private

Your nephew's shooting up between his toes, but he's not so stoned he
can't—on a tip from you—waste the cop who wasted his old man.

Next morning he visits his mother in her shitty house in Belleville.
Curlers and a bathrobe; a lukewarm cup of tea. He wonders: Does
she ever miss Dickie Moltisanti? She glances at the picture of the
long-gone man in a sailor's cap: *When he was in prison, or since he's
been dead?*

Revenge never tasted blander. Your nephew asks if she'll make him a
fluffernutter, but, no, she can't: she hasn't kept any peanut butter
since he left.

No Show

Down at the Riverfront Esplanade construction project in Newark,
the Other City by the Bay, wise guys shoot the shit in lawn chairs,
ignoring the forklifts and cranes, the hard-hatted morons doing real
work.

If a few things should go missing—a couple thousand feet of fiber optic
cable, for instance, or a load of Mexican travertine floor tiles—
insurance will cover it.

Somebody else always pays. You get your cut.

If only your aimless daughter were as easy to temper. She's been a no-
show all summer.

Still, she figures it out. Last day to sign up for classes at Columbia, she
pieces together a schedule, even scoring the ultimate creampuff:
"Philosophy: Morality, Self and Society."

No prerequisites.

Christopher

Members of the New Jersey Council of Indian Affairs and other assorted
rabble have hung an effigy of the High Admiral of the Sea from a
lamppost in Washington Park. "Mussolini was Hitler's Bitch!" they
shout at the Knights of Columbus, those brave defenders of the
faith.

The mob wives are getting even less respect at a lecture on "Italian
American Women and Pride." As if organized crime didn't have
its upsides. These Montclair State professors, what do they know
anyway?

You're the boss—you just want to make a dishonest buck, tuck into a
decent plate of rigatoni, maybe toss back a few glasses of not-too-
smoky Cabernet.

But pride infects your entire extended family, like smallpox on
Hispaniola: they won't stop yabbering and palavering about
injustice.

None of this ends well, you know: you watch the History Channel
practically every day.

The Weight

Johnny Sacramoni's enormous wife is ravenous. Forget about the
pasta and tomato sauce; we're talking crab cakes and crumb cakes
and Krispy Kreme donuts. She stashes Ho-Ho's and Skittles, Fig
Newtons and Twix and Milky Ways in an empty box of All in the
laundry room

It's hurtful, Johnny tells anyone who'll listen—the jocularity aimed at
these poor panguts—like watching your wife dance with another
man.

Ultimately, though, hunger is a bargain, like any other: *either name a
price, or get the fuck over it.*

Pie-O-My

If you knew your nephew's fiancée was flirting with the Feds, the junk
 they shoot, your sister's plans to snag another man, this singular
 moment would not exist.

Fortunately, you're blessed with ignorance.

Sitting in the stall of your fickle capo's ailing racehorse on a rainy night,
 you rub her chestnut hide, soothe her soft whinnying, breathe in the
 reassuring smells of cigar smoke and dried manure and fresh hay.

Tomorrow you'll collect outstanding debts. Not today.

Everybody Hurts

Driving through the Bronx, your son has a revelation: America's unfair: some people, they don't even have a dining room.

You have bigger concerns. Your ex-goomar, the Mercedes saleswoman, has hung herself, and no one bothered to let you know.

Then Artie Bucco's on the hook for fifty grand he loaned a French businessman. On the verge of suicide, he calls to say goodbye. Saved by you, he unloads on his savior.

People: those miserable fucks. They blame you when you're twenty moves ahead of them, but is that a cause for shame, or pride? If they had the gift of foresight, you can bet they'd find a way to abide their good luck.

Watching Too Much Television

Some people weep when they get sad. Not you. You belt-whip the
   assemblyman who's taken up with a long-ago goomar. *Cry,* you tell
   the man, huddled on the floor in his underwear, *cry like a bitch.*

It was the Chi-Lites on 101.1 that set you off: "Oh Girl."

You can scam HUD, strip the copper piping from dirty real estate, sell
   the very wall sconces from a house, but you can't escape the music of
   your youth.

Just look at the old neighborhood. Windows boarded up, trash strewn
   across the stoops and barren yards. Not a whiff of basil or oregano.

Listen, too, when your back is turned, to reruns on the idiot box:
   Murder, She Wrote and *Murder One* and *Diagnosis: Murder.* Odd
   harmonies in the theme music. Secrets in the dialogue.

Mergers and Acquisitions

Your wife leaves the sequin-tipped fake fingernail of your new goomar
    on the bedside table, next to your keys and change, your lighter and
    the crumpled wrapper of a stick of Wrigley's spearmint gum.

It's a declaration of war you're not yet ready to receive, though she's
    stolen twenty grand from the locked bin of birdfood in the
    backyard. Instead, you accept her offer of a cup of coffee—regular,
    not decaf.

Your capos are equally bedeviled: Ralph, whose masochistic predilections
    are becoming public; and Paulie, whose mother's making a fool
    of herself at the Green Grove retirement home—taking out her
    dentures in the middle of dinner, taking a hit on 18 on Monte Carlo
    Night.

Whoever Did This

Ralph Cifaretto had to go after he torched the stables, filling dawn with
the stench of charred wood and flesh: Pie-O-My shrouded in a tarp,
wrapped in chains—a tractor hauling her away.

What sick fuck thinks a racehorse is an occasion for an insurance scam?
We're talking about a beautiful innocent creature here, a fucking
living thing.

Afterwards, your nephew arrives with rubber gloves and bleach and
garbage bags to clean up the mess. Ever thorough, the two of you
hack off Ralph's hands and head with a meat cleaver, stash them in a
bowling ball bag.

While you wait for the body to bleed out in the bathtub, you eat peanut
butter from the jar with a knife and dispense avuncular advice: *Don't
overthink it.*

The Strong, Silent Type

Your nephew, shooting skag, nods off to *The Little Rascals*, beneath him
   on the couch his fiancee's Maltese, Cozette.

It's intervention time.

An interposal's also in order for your wife: if she doesn't stop flirting
   with Furio, the Sicilian heartthrob who drives you about your
   business, someone's blood will be shed.

And yet who can blame her for swooning over a man who grates his
   own Parmesan and broods over a glass of Nero d'Avola as though he
   were writing a poem.

Calling All Cars

The meaning is elicited through verbalization, your psychiatrist tells you. It's up to you to explain why you dream of sitting in the backseat of your father's Cadillac while your wife drives, a crucifix hanging from the rearview mirror, "Tears of a Clown" on the radio.

But life's too knotty for enodations. In the old days, a dream was just a fucking dream. It was always men in front, wives in back. Wives on Saturday nights, mistresses on Fridays. You whacked a guy, he stayed whacked.

Now, you can't interpret anything.

If dreams are wishes, what wish does your latest represent? You're in the country, on the porch of a large house, locusts shrilling. A stonemason in suspenders and a dirty shirt, hat clasped tightly in your hand, you rap on the door, which opens of itself to reveal a woman on the stairs, shadowed, yes, but surely the very image of your mother.

Eloise

You tell your wife your daughter has become a beautiful independent
woman. Isn't that all she ever wanted—to make a house and raise a
family, to take tea at the Plaza in white gloves with her little girl?

In bed, your heavy arm resting on her shoulder, she thinks of the man
she loves, whose very name means *to become furious.* She ought to
shed this comforter with a curse, dress and take a cab to JFK, follow
him to Sicily.

Instead she stares at the wallpaper pattern she chose all those years ago
and answers quietly but firmly, *Yes,* then closes her eyes, opens them,
then closes them again.

Whitecaps

You buy a beach house in Sea Bright, a big three-story place with its own dock and a rowboat in the yard. The name's spelled out on the front porch in three-strand rope, framed in seashells and starfish.

There ought to be a happy ending here, for once, but these Russian goomars, once dumped, can't leave well enough alone. She calls your wife, reveals everything the poor woman thought she already knew.

You have to forgo the vacation place, and soon you're moved into your own pool house, sleeping on a blow-up mattress while the Second World War plays on your home cinema.

Then you're out of North Caldwell altogether.

At least your nephew's clean. And rehab hasn't affected his knack for butchery one bit. He can still do his part in a double-hit while keeping the ash on his cigarette intact.

5

Two Tonys

Tony Blundetto, your killer cousin, is back from fifteen years in the can.
   You missed him, your unlucky doppelgänger: when you were kids,
   they dubbed you Tony Uncle Johnny, while he was Tony Uncle Al.

Also out are Feech La Manna and Angelo Garepe and Phil Leotardo,
   which probably isn't good.

Then your nephew and Paulie Gualtieri are feuding over who has to
   pick up the tab on goomar night: steaks and three-pound lobsters
   and a bottle of Cristal for the skanks at the next table. Fortunately,
   a thickheaded waiter follows them into the parking lot to complain
   about his tip. They waste him together—friends again.

You're free now to pursue your psychiatrist, with roses and cruise tickets
   and promises of reform. But she knows your secrets: she won't
   budge.

You go home to sit in darkness on your patio, autumn leaves skittering
   across the pool cover, an AK-47 between your legs—waiting for the
   return of the elusive creature that's been harassing your family for
   years: the last Eastern black bear in Essex County.

Puffing on your Bolívar, you don't look the least bit scared.

Rat Pack

Carmine Lupertazzi's still in his open casket when the brangling and
campling and bickerment starts. Who hung the Opus Dei medal on
Carmine's rosary? Who's boss now: Little Carmine or Johnny Sack?
How long until one faction spies an opening and attacks?

Jack Massarone's wearing a wire in his Museum of Science and Trucking
Cap. Your nephew's fiancée has started fingering those she doesn't
like. And Tony B. will surely make a mistake in the unfamiliar
straight world.

Sometimes you wonder how many people you're going to have to clip to
keep the *Stugots* sailing. It's like your uncle says: *Old rats on a new
ship.*

Where's Johnny?

Bobby Baccala has to spend forty minutes at Rite Aids picking up
    stool softener for your uncle. Truth is, you find that pretty fucking
    funny—any husband of your sister deserves a measure of grief.

Not so funny is your uncle's creeping dementia. *Small hands,* he tells
    you, *that was always your problem. A goddamn hothouse flower. No
    wonder you never played college ball.*

That's it: you're never eating Sunday dinner again with the undermining
    old fuck.

Junior could care less. Next day, he drives down to the old
    neighborhood—looking for Damiano, looking for his brother,
    Johnny Boy Soprano, dead now these ten years.

But no one knows those ghosts anymore, so he wanders up 14th Avenue
    in his overcoat and undershirt, an ancient fool who finally finds an
    empty bench on which to rest, the rain-wet ruins of Irvington before
    him like a cul-de-sac in Hell.

All Happy Families...

If your son could just pull his grades up to a "C," you'd be a proud papa, but, no, he's a lying sack of shit, that one, his face Krazy Glued to the carpet in a hotel room, his eyebrows shaved and drawn in with a Sharpie. Sure, his eyebrows will grow back, but what the fuck?

If only he were as easy to dispose of as Feech LaManna, that meddling buccaneer, whom you arrange to have sent back to Sing Sing for receiving stolen property. You gauged his greed correctly: another ten years of prison for a single flat screen TV.

Irregular Around the Margins

You could have fucked your nephew's sweetheart, if you weren't such a
  gentleman.

Okay, maybe you lingered against her a little too long during your game
  of darts. And the nighttime drive to score some coke was a definite
  mistake—that fucking raccoon in the middle of the road, the wreck,
  the uncertainty.

Now Bellville's buzzing with tittle and blab, and Kearny's awash in
  rumor.

All your unsteady dependencies are on the verge of crumbling, so you
  insist on a public dinner: you and your wife, your nephew and his
  fiancée. Everyone dressed to the nines and saving face.

Filling the silence between the clink of crystal and the clatter of
  silverware, an aria from *La Rondine: Who cares for wealth when there
  is happiness?*

Oh, golden dream!

Sentimental Education

Your wife finds a Penguin paperback in the bathroom of your son's guidance counselor: *The Letters of Abelard and Heloise*. Highlighted and annotated. She's naked, of course, smiling with sin. In bed, setting a high tone, he tells her an education should never end.

But it has to *begin* first: your idiot son, stumbling through high school, has plagiarized his paper on *Lord of the Flies*. Now the guidance counselor, this Abelard, is putting the screws on his fellow educators to get the kid to pass.

He can't do it for long. He admits he's guilt-prone, can't condone her sexual manipulation. They need to take a break.

Fuck you! You'd better watch your step, she tells him, struggling back into her dress, slamming the door, delivering a little enlightenment of her own.

In Camelot

In the hush of the Jersey City Cemetery, you come across your father's
old goomar, musing by his grave. Fran Felstein. Well turned out.
Great legs for an old broad. She says she doesn't need a thing.

But she's unsettled after all these years, cheated out of her share of the
midget raceway down in New Egypt, barely able to pay her phone
bill, this woman who once partied with JFK.

You'd worship her, the elegant mother you never had, but she's a
spendthrift, impetuous, really just a high-class whore. Turns out
she smoked like a house afire, though your father was dying of
emphysema, though even your self-obssessed mother quit.

Then there's that buried memory you're just now dredging up: your
mother's miscarriage, how you spent the night with her at the
hospital while your father made merry with Fran Felstein. You lied
about it to cover your old man—that handsome, treacherous son of a
bitch, long rotted in the grave.

Marco Polo

At your father-in-law's seventy-fifth, you preside again over your own
home, grilling sausages from Palumbo's, cracking dirty jokes.

Your gift: a Berretta DT-10 over-under. The old gent couldn't be more
pleased.

Later, lit by underwater lights, you play pool games with your wife.

Next morning, the backyard's a suburban battlefield: empty Heinekens,
plastic cups and paper plates, helium balloons drifting like the
ghosts of soldiers, half-deflated beach balls floating in the tepid
water.

A barking dog awakes you. As she sleeps, you slip from your marriage
bed.

Unidentified Black Males

Tony B. whacked Joey Peeps, and that's the best alibi he can conjure?
   Come on: he can only play that poor-me, ex-con cousin card so
   long. The fucking *gabadotz* has pissed on a bees' nest.

On top of that, your wife won't stop with the divorce shit, even though
   you sent her flowers after your tryst, and even a little note, saying it
   was nice.

You may be a robot to your own pussy-assed lunacies, but you're still the
   boss. It's like you tell your daughter's boyfriend when the kid tries
   picking up the tab at the Old Homestead Steakhouse: *You eat. I pay.*

Cold Cuts

Revenge is like serving cold cuts, and that's exactly what Johnny Sack is offering up. He stole a cargo container of Vespa scooters right off the Hackensack River, and he'll do the same with that shipment of imported provolone. In fact, he'll keep on skewering New Jersey until the death of Joey Peeps is avenged.

Things aren't much better up in Kinderhook. Uncle Pat is selling off his farm, where half the missing mobsters from the Garden State are buried. All night your nephew and Tony B. shovel corpses, breaking bones and scooping them into gunnysacks.

Meanwhile, your sister's taking anger management classes after pummeling the face of another soccer mom. She's making progress, avoiding conflict, not losing her shit when Bobby's kids leave their bikes in the middle of the driveway.

Unfortunately, her progress doesn't last long. The family temper's legendary.

The Test Dream

It's a test you're sure to fail eventually: sacrificing your own best interests
for those of someone else.

So you dream through the night in your suite at the Plaza: wind in the
branches on a cobblestone street; your teeth falling out, clattering on
an empty plate.

Then your footsteps echo through the empty halls of Clifton High as
you make your way past the mirrored trophy case. Coach Molinaro,
that cigar-chomping brute of a man you always disappointed, waits
in his office, ready to break your balls.

When you finally wake, it's too late. Tony B. has made the hit. Billy
Leotardo's dying in his brother's arms.

Long Term Parking

The FBI has squeezed your nephew's wife-to-be until she's ready to scream. They want her to flip *now*. They want you.

They insist your nephew renounce everything, and he thinks about it, he sincerely does: he loves her that much.

Then you, the man she's counted as a friend for years, call to say he's swallowed a bottle of pills in Ramapo: he was depressed about something, you don't know what. Another friend will be by momentarily to drive her to the hospital.

She accepts the ride, though surely she must know she'll end up in the silent autumn woods, two bullets to the brain.

Surely, she's known that all along.

Your nephew drives her Thunderbird to the long term parking lot, weeping but resolute, because mobsters are strong, they're resilient that way. He leaves the car there in the light rain, where it will be weeks before the airport authority realizes it no longer belongs to anyone.

All Due Respect

After you shoot your cousin with a shotgun on the porch of your uncle's
house, it's comforting to come back to the Bada Bing! for a cup of
coffee and a bialy, with extra poppy seeds and onions.

You escape from the FBI raid on Johnny Sack's place by wading through
knee-deep snow, crossing a creek in your dress shoes, tearing your
thousand dollar overcoat on the branch of a locust tree.

Your solicitous wife welcomes you home.

Be of good cheer, your lawyer tells you. *You weren't named in the
indictment.* The bear's in hibernation. Phil Leotardo's walking with
a cane.

Dry your eyes.

6.1

Members Only

It's the Year of the Rat.

Buffalo Ray Curto dies of a stroke while talking to his handler.

Then Gene Pontecorvo's dangling from the rafters in his basement. That
dream he had of leaving your crew and retiring to Florida? He had
to let it go.

Finally, your uncle, living in and out of time, shoots you in the gut.
Cazzata Malanga! he shouts before running upstairs and hiding in
the closet.

Most men would shut their eyes and die, but you'll do anything to save
yourself. Bleeding, you crawl across the living room floor, panting,
sweating, moaning. You pull yourself up the wall, dial 9-1-1, black
out.

On the phonograph, it's Artie Shaw and his band. Helen Forest singing
"Comes Love."

Join the Club

There's a hole in your chest the size of New Jersey, but you're deep in a coma, living another life as a salesman for an optics manufacturer. Your new self is stuck in Costa Mesa—some other fat man has walked away with your I.D.

Back in Newark, your actual family's disintegrating. Your wife hasn't left the hospital in days. Sweat-suited, hair unwashed, make-up unattended to, she sits by your bed, listening to you wheeze into your breathing tube.

Your associates feign concern, but the question of succession looms. People die. A man still has to earn.

In California, that land of the near-dead, it's a whole new world. *Who am I?* you ask, as a helicopter hovers over you in the Omni parking lot, its searchlight bright as a surgeon's headlamp. *Where am I going?*

Mayham

Chaos descends.

Silvio's a shitty acting boss. He gets asthma attacks just deciding how to
split the take from a shootout with the Columbians.

Vito Spatafore's got his eye on *capo di tutti*, though everyone hates his
tub of (albeit diminishing) guts.

And Paulie Gualtieri, sitting by your hospital bed, complains so
loudly of his own eyes, teeth and *coglioni,* it penetrates your coma:
tachycardia, thready pulse. *Grab the paddles! Clear the room!*

In that dark place where spirits cross and re-cross the threshold, there's a
party for the dead. Music. A large house festooned with lights. The
cousin whose brains you splattered across Kinderhook is smiling,
inviting you to put your business down.

But you're not ready yet to go inside. A voice is calling from the wind-
blown woods: *Daddy, we love you. Don't leave us. Daddy, don't go!*

The Fleshy Part of the Thigh

Though your recovery's in motion, your subordinates continue to
    whirl about like tornados, or molecules clouting one another in the
    universal soup.

A rapper pays Bobby Baccala seven grand to shoot him—street cred
    for his next CD. No marksman, Bobby misses his target, hits poor
    Marvin in the ass instead.

Paulie Gualtieri learns his aunt—a nun knocked up during the War—is
    really his mother. He wants no part of her deathbed confession.
    Later, he tells the woman who raised him he never wants to see her
    again.

Out of the hospital, you swear to your sister that every day is now a gift.
    But look at you there in your pajamas, settling into a lawn chair in
    your backyard. The same wind that coursed through your brain
    that night you nearly died is here in North Caldwell on a sunny
    afternoon—the trees shivering, the surface of the swimming pool
    like ripples starting on the Sea of Galilee.

Mr. & Mrs. John Sacrimoni Request...

Your former partner in crime has six hours at his daughter's four
 hundred thousand dollar wedding. The wedding guests are legion,
 including a contingent of U. S. Marshalls for which he has to pay.
 Johnny Sack's a real stand-up guy in his tuxedo and boutonnière...
 until his time is up. When they cuff and shove him into a waiting
 SUV, he weeps like an old woman to leave his little girl.

The other mobsters call it fucking disgraceful behavior. But you, a man
 recently acquainted with death's drear family, know different: when
 it comes to daughters, all bets are off.

Still, better to be stouthearted, even if you must thrash a member of
 your own crew to remind everyone who's boss. Afterwards, bent
 over the toilet, you smile at your valor while vomiting blood into the
 bowl.

Live Free or Die

All this time, Vito Spatofore's been as queer as a plaid *coniglio*. So says
   Sal Iacuzzo from Yonkers, and the proof is Vito fleeing.

Now he's holed up in a B & B in the Granite State, pretending to be a
   writer.

The guy's representing you and your crew, the honor of the family, but
   you don't want a rush to judgment—he's a great earner. Without
   Vito, you might not have your new three million dollar boat.

After a chat with your shrink, you recommend mercy—up to a point, of
   course.

And Vito? He's cruising the quaint main street of Dartford, where he
   has a natural eye for quality antiques. That Baneda vase he just
   picked up? It's the most expensive piece in the store.

Luxury Lounge

Little Carmine and your nephew, Cecil B. DeMoltisanti, take a meeting
with Sir Ben Kingsley in LA, but he has no interest in starring in a
mob-financed picture, much less one entitled *Cleaver*.

Nevertheless, the two follow him into the luxury lounge. A White &
Warm cashmere throw, a classic stainless Oris chrono, champagne,
sunglasses, shoes, headphones—they are literally giving this shit
away.

Not to gangsters, though, and your nephew feels it in his gut: this sense
paesani always have around nobility: somebody's getting rich sitting
on his ass while others are doing the hard work.

A few days later, he steals Lauren Bacall's gift bag after punching her in
the face.

Johnny Cakes

Your son's slacking from his job at Blockbuster so he can sit home on the
   couch and watch *Aqua Teen Hunger Force*. Master Shake, Frylock,
   Meatwad: that's about where his head's at now.

In New Hampshire, Vito's finally found love: a short order frycook and
   volunteer fireman named Jim. If you saw them kissing, shirtless, by
   a pond, you'd probably sympathize with Phil Leotardo, who wants
   his *finook* cousin dead.

Your own voracious *cazzo* is also causing problems—some realtor who
   wants to buy Caputo's Poultry and turn it into a Jamba Juice. Your
   conscience sends you home unsated this time, but you rage in the
   kitchen at your faithful, astounded wife: *What does it take to get some*
   fucking smoked turkey in this house?

The Ride

Paulie Gualtieri's in charge of the annual Feast of Saint Elzéar of Sabran:
therefore, no expense will be borne than can reasonably be shirked:
security, electric, sanitation. Of course, the street fair will offer
zeppole, calzone, pizza by the slice, but fuck the saint's gold hat—
Father José wants too much this year.

And then the teacup ride—a bolt busted, the thing jammed, and all
because Paulie wouldn't pay for maintenance. Now there's a major
rumpus between him and Bobby Baccala. It's up to you to broker a
ceasefire.

Someday this cheap fuck is going to cost you big, so thank God for the
vision Paulie has in the Bada Bing!—the Virgin Mary floating above
the stage between the strippers' poles.

When she's gone, it's enough to reconcile him to his adopted mother.
They sit silently together in her room and watch *Lawrence Welk* on
Channel 55: Bobby and Sissy dancing to the "Johnny Oslo Shadish"
in Norwegian attire.

Moe n' Joe

You hate your sister, that uncanny incarnation of your mother. She's
    right: there's nothing holding you together but DNA.

Her husband is despised by his adolescent son, who no longer wants
    to waste time on model railroading in the garage. The woodland
    mountain with a twenty-seven inch peak? The Moe n' Joe action,
    two tiny figures dumping miniature slats of wood into a train car?
    He's got more important things to do, like watching his friends
    make a music video.

Vito and Johnny Cakes will never be happier in their cozy cabin—pasta
    patana and vinegar peppers and unending sex—but the action in
    New England is for shit. Vito packs without saying goodbye, is
    soon back slouching in the shadows of Clifton and Kearny.

And to no one's surprise, you've found a way to profit from Johnny
    Sack's misfortune—that thing with the fuckheads from fuckland.
    By your own admission, whatever happens, you only have yourself
    to blame.

Cold Stones

There's nothing gay about hell, Patty Leotardo tells her husband, Phil, and
that turns out to be the case. He and two goons ambush Vito in the
Courtesy Motel in Fort Lee. Duct tape and iron pipes. A pool cue
up his ass.

Even Paris, where your wife has gone to repair her tattered soul, turns
out to be less carefree than she'd imagined. Marble angels on the
storefronts, the icy nave of Saint-Eustache, crumbling Roman baths,
cobblestone bridges over the Seine—so many lives, she thinks, and it
all gets washed away.

In a dream, she meets the ghost of your nephew's fiancée, walking her
dog in the Tuileries. She smiles, the lovely, unquick woman you had
killed.

If you're not dead, you must still be alive.

Kaisha

You don't have to eat every plate of Rigatoni, your psychiatrist tells you,
   but look what your fucking turkey neck of a nephew did the last
   time you passed up a dish: he's banging that realtor now, the one
   you couldn't bring yourself to do: reminding you of the unpleasant
   fact you don't get everything you want.

This Christmas it's hard to parse your plight. Your daughter's in
   California, and your son's new girlfriend is ten years older than him,
   has a kid, is Dominican—*maybe.*

As your fickle family gathers around the towering tree piled high with
   gifts, a dismal drone thrums just beneath "O Holy Night."

6.2

Soprano Home Movies

Bobby Baccala doesn't cheat at Monopoly, the fucking crybaby. And now you make a harmless joke about your sister having some guy's schlong in her mouth. That's it: he punches you, and then the two of you are charging around his lake house, grappling like bull moose in rutting season, knocking over lamps and chairs, demolishing the coffee table.

Defeated, you lie on your back, a plastic hotel stuck to your bloody cheek.

His punishment for winning is his first hit: a scumbag in Montréal. The cherry popping's overdue, of course, after all these years.

Back home, you watch the DVD your sister burned of some old Super 8s: the two of you washing your father's Cadillac at the house on New York Avenue. She squirts you in the face with the hose. You run down the street chasing her.

Stage 5

Johnny Sack's stage 4 small cell carcinoma of the lungs has metastasized to his mediastinal lymph nodes, both kidneys and his brain. The lobectomy, radiation, chemo: what was it all for? Kicks?

Like Johnny, you wonder what sort of image you'll leave to the world. Some asshole bully in a bathrobe, the way your nephew portrays you in his gangster horror movie?

When he was born, you used to hold him in your arms, and now this betrayal. Aren't you a good mentor? A loyal friend?

Just look at all you've done for him.

Remember When

Ah, *marone*, will Paulie Gualtieri never shut his fucking yap? The Feds have dug up Willie Overall, the first man you ever shot. Just in case, the two of you drive down to Miami.

It's all nostalgia with Paulie: your father's '59 Eldorado Biarritz with the fins, Mickey Pinto back in '63, that house on the shore with the bedbugs, summer of '78.

Finally, you shut him up: *"Remember when" is the lowest form of conversation.*

But even after they pin Willie's murder on someone else, you can't help thinking Paulie, with all his blather, is a liability.

Out on a rented boat, the *Sea Vous Play*, the knife you used for cutting chum is in your hand. In the swell, you weigh the consequences, along with the handle's heft, but the moment's wrong, or, more precisely, isn't right.

Chasing It

You can't catch a break: roulette, the ponies, Buffalo against Tampa Bay.

You're into Hesh Rabkin for two hundred grand. Old friend though he is, at what point is it cheaper just to pop him?

He knows it, too: these Italians, corner them and they're no more than animals.

The world, though, is watching. It wants to believe in a man with diamond cufflinks and a Salvatore Ferragamo tie.

You pay.

Walk Like a Man

You feel bad for your son, but how long can this pity party for his ex-girlfriend last? He's lying on the couch watching *Tom and Jerry* when he should be out banging co-eds.

Your nephew, too, that *donnicciola*, continues mooning over his ratfuck fiancée, justly rotting in the woods of Sussex County. He's like a ghost since he quit drinking, but liquored up, he's even worse: he shoots his sponsor when he wants to kill his rival, Paulie.

It's the most enduring truth in the underworld: a coward with a gun is still deadly.

Kennedy and Heidi

Heidi's driving after dark with just a learner's permit, so she tells
    Kennedy they'd better keep going after the accident.

Meanwhile, your Escalade is at the bottom of a ravine. You were
    wearing your seat belt; your nephew wasn't. He's bleeding, high—
    he'll never pass a drug test. He'll never pass any kind of test you
    administer.

Steely-eyed, you suffocate him.

You tell your shrink you're prostate with grief, but you admit his loss is a
    great relief: he was a tremendous drag on you.

Later, in Las Vegas to recuperate from your guilt, you swallow a button
    of peyote: you've murdered friends and relatives before, but this is
    something altogether different. Laughing and crying, you shout at
    the desert sunrise: *I get it!*

The Second Coming

Your son finally succumbs to the rough beast: he ties a cinder block to
    his leg, puts a plastic bag over his head, and drops into the deep end
    of your swimming pool.

Inevitably, the rope's too long to drag him down, and you come home in
    time to save him.

The stupid fuck. He had it all: a nice home, Lexapro, your wife's
    cooking. Now he's checked into the psych ward, and they won't
    even let you bring him pizza.

The Blue Comet

Then the hit on that *faccia di merda* Phil Leotardo goes wrong: North Jersey is at war with Brooklyn.

Silvio's in a coma after a shootout at the Bada Bing! Bobby Baccala's been gunned down in a hobby store, buying a toy train.

To top it off, your shrink is dropping you. You've been manipulating her for years, she claims, perfecting the art of sociopathy. She crosses her arms in her grey suit, opens the door until you leave.

Sequestered in a safehouse—the world you made no more substantial than a communion wafer—you sleep with an AK-47 across your chest.

Made in America

You never know when something will be over.

Phil Leotardo, for instance, is buying gas at a Raceway station in
Clifton, when he's shot in the head then crushed by his own car.

Your uncle's wheelchair-bound. He's lost his teeth, his memory.

Carlo Gervasi's turned rat: he's set to testify against you, and he's seen
more than enough.

At Holsten's Deli, you put Journey on the jukebox. Your family's
gathered round for the best onion rings in the state. *Focus on the
good times,* your son recalls you saying once.

You ring the bell for service, look up

David Starkey served as Santa Barbara's 2009-2010 Poet Laureate and is Director of the Creative Writing Program at Santa Barbara City College. He has published seven full-length collections of poetry, most recently *Circus Maximus* (Biblioasis, 2013) and *It Must Be Like the World* (Pecan Grove, 2011). In addition, over the past twenty-eight years he has published more than 400 poems in literary journals, including *American Scholar, Antioch Review, Georgia Review, Massachusetts Review,* and *Southern Review. Creative Writing: Four Genres in Brief* (Bedford/ St. Martin's, 2012) is in its second edition and is currently one of the best-selling creative writing textbooks in the country. The editor of numerous academic anthologies, Starkey is also the editor and publisher of Gunpowder Press.

Made in the USA
Charleston, SC
18 January 2015